The Story of God's Glorious Plan for Man

Cherri Campbell

The Story of God's Glorious Plan for Man
Copyright © 2019 by Cherri Campbell
Victorious Faith Publishing

All rights reserved. No part of this book may be reproduced or used in any manner whatsoever without the express written permission of the publisher except for the use of brief quotations in a book review.

Bold type in the scripture quotations indicates the author's emphasis. Pronouns referring to the Father, Son, and Holy Spirit are capitalized while the name satan and related names are not capitalized. We choose not to acknowledge him, even to the point of violating grammatical rules.

All Scripture quotations, unless otherwise indicated, are taken from the Holy Bible, New International Version®, NIV®. Copyright ©1973, 1978, 1984, 2011 by Biblica, Inc.™ Used by permission of Zondervan. All rights reserved worldwide. The "NIV" and "New International Version" are trademarks registered in the United States Patent and Trademark Office by Biblica, Inc.™

Scripture quotations marked (KJV) are taken from the authorized King James Version Bible.

Scripture quotations marked (AMPC) are taken from the Amplified Bible, Classic Edition. Copyright © 1954, 1958, 1962, 1964, 1965, 1987 by The Lockman Foundation. Used by permission. All rights reserved.

Scripture quotations marked (BBE) are taken from the 1949/1964 The Bible in Basic English, public domain.

Scripture quotations marked (NAB) are taken from the New American Bible. Copyright © 1991, 1986, 1970 by the Confraternity of Christian Doctrine, Washington, D.C., and are used by permission of the copyright owner. All Rights Reserved.

Scripture quotations marked (NAS) are taken from the New American Standard Bible, © Copyright The Lockman Foundation 1960, 1962, 1963, 1968, 1971, 1972, 1973, 1975, 1977, 1988, 1995. Used by permission. All rights reserved.

Scripture quotations marked (NET) are taken from the New English Translation (NET Bible, Version 1.0). Copyright © 1996–2018 by Biblical Studies Press, L.L.C. Used by permission. All rights reserved.

Scripture quotations marked (NKJV) are taken from the New King James Version®. Copyright © 1982 by Thomas Nelson. Used by permission. All rights reserved.

Scripture quotations marked (NLT) are taken from the Holy Bible, New Living Translation, Copyright ©1996, 2004, 2015 by Tyndale House Foundation. Used by permission of Tyndale House Publishers, Inc., Carol Stream, Illinois 60188. All rights reserved.

Scripture quotations marked Wuest translation are taken from The New Testament: An Expanded Translation by Kenneth S. Wuest. Copyright © 1961 by Wm. B. Eerdmans Publishing Company, Grand Rapids, MI. Used by permission. All rights reserved.

Victorious Faith Publishing
info@victoriousfaith.co

ISBN: 978-1-951800-00-0 (Paperback)

Contents

Chapter One

Creation

Let's start at the beginning. Before there was anything, there was God. God was before the beginning. God always was, and God began the beginning! Genesis 1:1 says:

> *"In the beginning, God created the heavens and the earth."*

As we understand from the Word of God, it seems the first thing God made, just before or after He made the heavens and the earth in Genesis 1:1, were the angels. Job 38:4–7 say:

> *4 "Where were you when I laid the earth's foundation? Tell me, if you understand.*
> *5 Who marked off its dimensions? Surely you know! Who stretched a measuring line across*
> *it? 6 On what were its footings set, or who*

> *laid its cornerstone—[7] while the morning stars sang together* ***and all the angels shouted for joy****?"*

(Many translations of the Bible translate "angels" as "sons of God," but the Septuagint—the Greek translation of the Hebrew Old Testament—and many other translations translate it "angels" because the angels were also called the "sons of God" in the Old Testament.)

So the angels were probably created before Genesis 1:1, or between Genesis 1:1–2, and satan fell between verses one and two (he was already fallen when God created man on the sixth day). There is a timeless period there. Angels were already in existence before man was created on the sixth day. Satan was an angel of God in heaven before he sinned and was cast down to earth (Ezekiel 28:11-17), and he was cast to earth before Adam was created.

The angels were with God when He made everything else, and they were created to be servants. Hebrews 1:14 says:

> *"Are not all angels ministering spirits sent to serve those who will inherit salvation?"*

Now let's just imagine what might have

happened, or what it might have been like during Creation as the angels watched. As it says in Job 38:7, *"all the angels shouted for joy!"*

God was working with all of His angels around Him, and He said, "Light be!" and light was. (That's the way it's written in the original Hebrew text in Genesis 1:3.) The angels might have said, "Oo-oo-oo!" When God made galaxy clusters, they might have said, "O-o-o-o-h!" And when He made nebulas they might have said, "Wow, God! That's cool! Do it again, God! Do it again!" (Now remember, we're just imagining what it might have been like to watch Creation. I'm looking forward to watching a replay of that!) The angels watched in amazement and wonder at all the things that He made.

God made the heavens, He made the earth, and then He brought forth the plants and trees on the earth, and then He made the fish, birds, and animals. When God made all these things, *He had the picture in His mind* exactly what He wanted so that when He wanted a dog, He made one that *looked exactly like the picture* He had in His mind. If the dog He saw in His mind had one head, four legs, and one tail, then when He created that dog, it did not have two heads, six legs, and three tails. No, it looked *exactly like the picture* He had. Where was the picture? In His mind.

Made in the Image of God

However, when God made man, He did *not* have a picture in His mind. It says in Genesis 1:26 (KJV), when God made man, He said:

> *"Let us make man in* **our** *image, after* **our** *likeness."*

"Image" is another word for "picture," so you could say, "in our picture." So what was He saying? He said, "I, God, will be the picture of man." He didn't have the picture *in* Him. God Himself *was* the picture of man. He was saying, "I will be the picture of what man is to look like." So you could say it like this: God was the original and man was the photocopy!

I want you to see that we are very much like God. You were created in His image. God does not look like an elephant with six arms. It is a sad thing to see in different parts of the world some people worship sharks, snakes, alligators, cows, elephants, or other animals and to see that they are worshipping something which is below them in status because *only man was created in the image of God*, not animals. We look like God. So, if you want to know what God looks like, look in the mirror!

Of course, we all have different features—different eyes, ears, nose, mouth, hair, etc. I don't look exactly like you, and you don't look exactly like me, but we all look like humans. Also, God has His own special facial features that make Him unique, but He is in the same form as you and me. We are in the same form as God.

I can prove that to you. Look at Colossians 1:15. Speaking of Jesus it says:

> *"The Son is the…"*

What?

> *"…the image…"*

Isn't that the same word we saw in Genesis 1:26?

> *"Let us make man in our* ***image****."*

Colossians 1:15 says:

> *"The Son is the* ***image*** *of the invisible God, the firstborn over all creation."*

The Amplified Bible (AMPC) says:

> *"He is the* ***exact likeness*** *of the unseen God [the visible representation of the invisible]…"*

So, Jesus is the exact image and likeness of God. If you want to know *exactly* what God looks like, then look at Jesus. Jesus was a man, just like you and me. That proves that God is like you and me.

We see the word "image" again in another verse. Second Corinthians 4:4 says:

> *"The god of this age has blinded the minds of unbelievers, so that they cannot see the light of the gospel that displays the glory of Christ,* ***who is the image of God.****"*

Again it says Christ is the image of God!

Someone said to me once that God is bigger than the universe. Yes, that is true. The earth is His footstool (Isaiah 66:1). That is another mystery. We cannot answer the questions: "How can God live in us and we live in Him? How can He be everywhere at the same time?" Because He is God! That is why He can be everywhere at the same time. So we don't understand how He can be the size of a man and yet fill the whole universe, but He is because Jesus really is the image of God!

Let me prove it with another scripture. Hebrews 1:3 says:

> *"The Son is the radiance of God's glory and the exact representation of his being...."*

This says that Jesus, the Son of God, is the exact representation of God! That does not mean he is a little bit like God—he is the *exact* representation of God! Jesus was a man and he looks like a man, just like you and me; *and* he is the image of God, and the exact representation of His being. So we know again that we are made in the image of God!

I will give you one more verse. Isaiah 40:12 (NAS) says:

> *"Who has measured the waters in the hollow of His hand, And marked off the heavens by the span, And calculated the dust of the earth by the measure, And weighed the mountains in a balance, And the hills in a pair of scales?"*

Of course, this is speaking about God. This is the greatness of God! God measured the waters in the hollow of His hand. He took a drop of water and weighed the Pacific Ocean, the Atlantic Ocean, the Indian Ocean, all the seas, all the lakes, and all the rivers. He measured the rainfall and evaporation and the tides, and He made them come into perfect balance. By the dust of the earth, He weighed the mountains. Just think about that. This is the God who planned your life! Don't you think He can handle your problems?

Now let's look at this phrase, *"marked off the heavens by the span."* The New King James Version (NKJV) says, *"Measured heaven with a span."* A span is the distance from the tip of the little finger to the tip of the thumb when the hand is fully spread. That was used as a measurement in ancient times—they would measure things by their hand. The dictionary says a span is nine inches. The Amplified Bible (AMPC) also says *"a nine-inch span,"* so it is specific about the size of that span.

I have taken a ruler into the classroom at different times and passed it around the class, and I have found that at least half of the men in the class have a nine-inch span, showing that an average man's hand has a nine-inch span. So that means God's hand is the same size as the average man's hand. Jesus was an average size man. One time there was a tall man in the class who has long fingers, and I asked him to measure his hand. He had a ten-inch span. I jokingly said, "Your hand is bigger than God's!" I want you to see how much we are like God. We are in the image of God!

Creative Ability

Think about how we build buildings, design airplanes, design computer programs for space exploration, and we get new inventions. What is that? That is the creativity of God. God put in us

His creative ability to write music and books, draw paintings, and build things. Animals cannot do that. Why? Because they do not have that creative ability, and neither do the angels. *We were given the same ability as God to create, to have ideas, to dream, to vision, and to plan*! Animals don't plan what they're going to do next week or five years from now. But we plan, we build buildings, we build cities, we expand, we conquer, and we have the desire inside of us to explore. Why does mankind want to explore the universe? Because we were created in the image and likeness of God! We were created with His creative ability and the desire to conquer and have dominion!

Why Did God Make Mankind?

God created mankind for a purpose. What was that purpose? Most Christians will say God made mankind for two reasons—to worship Him and to serve Him. But that cannot be correct because He already had the angels. The Bible says God has *"many angels, numbering thousands upon thousands, and ten thousand times ten thousand"* (Revelation 5:11), and they were created to worship Him and serve Him. If God had already created the angels to worship and serve Him, then He did not need to create mankind to do the same thing. So that cannot be the main purpose for mankind.

There is a much more important reason—a much more wonderful reason!

God made mankind because God is Love! Love is never satisfied until it is expressed and shared with someone who can give it back, so God wanted to share love and fellowship. That's why the Bible says He walked with Adam in the garden in the cool of the day (Genesis 3:8), why He called Abraham His friend (Isaiah 41:8; James 2:23), why He said He talked to Moses face to face (Exodus 33:11), and why He said David was a man after His own heart (Acts 13:22). He wanted fellowship! He wanted a family!

Yes, you can pour your love on your little puppy, and it will lick you all over your face, but it cannot have an intelligent conversation with you. It cannot share your dreams and your vision.

When God made man in His image, He made him because He wanted fellowship, and He wanted to give and receive love. That is why He made *you*. It was for love and fellowship. He wants to talk to *you* face to face! He wants to walk with you in the cool of the day. He wants to call *you* His friend! He wants you to be a man or woman after His own heart. He wants that fellowship, that relationship, just like we need fellowship and relationship. And He is waiting for you to say to Him, "I love you, Father! I love you, Jesus!"

So, you were created to be the object of God's love. Wow! Isn't that good? Say, "Lord, just pour it on! If you made me just so you could love me, then pour it on because I'm here! I love you! I return it back to you. I say to you, Father, I love you! I love you! I love you!" Then you can just sit there quietly and hear Him say, "I love you, too!"[1]

We were made by Love Himself, for love. First of all, to have love and fellowship with God, and second, to have love and fellowship with each other. Mankind is the only creature created for the purpose of love! We need love as much as we need food. Without love, we have no purpose or value in life. There are people who will commit suicide because they think no one loves them. Did you ever see a dog walking around with its head down saying, "I'm going to kill myself because nobody loves me?" No. Animals don't need love. They are content even with no love, but man doesn't want to live another day without love.

We need love every day. That's why you need to say, "I love you" to your family. Those are not weak words. They are very strong words. A weak, selfish, and proud person has a hard time saying those words. It's a strong person who says it and means it. It takes strength and faith. It takes self-sacrifice, unselfishness, and humility to say, "I love you" and truly mean it—not to get something, but to give something to another person. The Lord said to me one time, *"The most important thing in life and the only thing that counts is loving people (and God)!"*

Angels were not created in the image of God, so they don't need love either. I don't know a scripture that says God loves the angels, or that He tells them He loves them, or that He lays down His life for them. But God told His people,

> *"…I have loved you with an everlasting love"* (Jeremiah 31:3)

And Jesus told his disciples in John 15:9:

> *"As the Father has loved me, so have I loved you…"*

And in John 10:11 he said,

> *"I am the good shepherd. The good shepherd lays down his life for the sheep."*

God has said He loves us over and over and over again!

Another thing about the angels is that because they're servants, they do as they're told, and they say exactly what they're told to say. They don't have the freedom of choice and free will to choose their words. Gabriel comes with a message, but he does not come with his own words. He only comes with God's words.

What if someone just repeats what you tell them to say, and so they say, "I love you" because you told them to? Does that make you feel really good and warm? No. There is no heartbeat in it, is there?

But what if your little two-year-old daughter crawls up in your lap, puts her hands on your face, and says, "Mommy/Daddy, I love you!" Or your eighteen-year-old son says, "I love you, Dad/Mom!" Does that melt your heart? Yes, it does! Why? Because that person can choose to say, "I love you!" They have both the freedom of choice and the capacity to give and express love, so it deeply touches your heart!

In the same way, God wanted someone who could freely choose to receive and give His love! When God made us in His own image, He made us with free choice *and* with His capacity to express love, as well as with the ability to have intelligent conversation with Him, sharing His dreams and vision! Glory to God!

Another reason God made us in His own image is that God wanted children who could rule and reign with Him. God does not want His work to be called, "God, Inc." It is supposed to be "God & Sons, Inc."! God doesn't only want servants around Him. He wants children who rule with Him! Praise the Lord! He wants love, fellowship, *and family*!

Chapter Two

When God created man in His own image, He created him with three things: position (or rank), authority, and glory.

Position

In Psalm 8:3–4 it says:

> [3] *"When I consider your heavens, the work of your fingers, the moon and the stars, which you have set in place,* [4] *what is mankind that you are mindful of them, human beings that you care for them?"*

To understand this better, let's look at Hebrews 1:14:

> *"Are not all angels ministering spirits sent to serve those who will inherit salvation?"*

Hebrews chapter two continues speaking about angels, as you see in verses two and five.

(Many times people think a chapter break means there is a change of subject, but that is often not the case. The chapter and verse numbers were added much later than the original text was written. Therefore, we have to continue reading from one chapter into the next to continue the thought and to understand the context of the whole passage.)

So chapter two is still talking about angels. Hebrews 2:5–6 (NKJV) say:

> 5 *"For He has not put the world to come, of which we speak, in subjection to* ***angels.***
> 6 ***But one testified in a certain place, saying:*** *What is man that You are mindful of him, Or the son of man that You take care of him?"*

Verse six says there is one who "testified." One what? The context is about the angels, so there was one angel who said this. And then it quotes Psalm 8:4–6. So we know it was an angel who was speaking.

Now let us go back to our dialogue. Psalm 8:3–4 say:

> 3 *"When I consider your heavens, the work of your fingers, the moon and the stars, which you have set in place,* 4 *what is man…?"*

The angels were watching God create the stars, and they were saying, "Oo-oo-oo! Ahhhh! Wow!" Then God made man, saying, *"Let us make man in our image"* (Genesis 1:26). He made this man in His own image, and the angels were standing back looking at this man, looking at God, looking at the man, looking at God. They noticed these two looked alike. (Jesus is called the last Adam in 1 Corinthians 15:45, so I believe the first Adam looked just like Jesus, who is the image of God!)

I like to think of it like this (Cherri's version): One angel whispered to another, "What is man?" The other angel said, "I don't know. Ask him." They started asking each other, "What is man?" "I don't know. Try asking him." "Hey, what is man?" "I don't know. You had better ask God." "I'm not asking God, you ask God." "I'm not asking God, you ask God." Then one angel got the courage and boldness to go up to God and said, "Excuse me, God. Can I ask you a question? What is man?"

I like to imagine His answer like this: If you are getting ready to have a special guest come to your home, you make all the preparations, get the room ready, and get the bed ready. And if somebody is watching what you're doing, they might ask you, "What are you doing? What is this for?" You might answer them, "Just wait and see."

All the preparations are being made because someone special is coming.

Or what if you are expecting a baby? You get a baby's room ready with a crib, dresser, baby clothes, and blankets, etc.

Well, what did God create last? Mankind. So that means everything else that He made first was getting the room ready! He got the earth ready. He made the stars for us to look at—like a mobile hanging above a baby's crib for the baby to look up at—and the sun and moon to give us light and warmth. He put all the water in place; He made the flowers, the fish, the birds, and the animals, and got everything ready. Then He made man in His own image, and said, "Man, this is yours." Psalm 115:16 says:

> *"The highest heavens belong to the Lord, but the earth he has given to mankind."*

So that means God made the earth for mankind. God made the earth for *you*! It was made for us. It was designed with us in mind!

And so the angels were watching and wondering, "What is all this preparation for? Who is this person? What is this man?" And we read the question in Psalm 8:4:

> *"What is mankind that you are mindful of them, human beings that you care for them?"*

In other words, "Why are you doing all these things, and who is this man?"

Then Psalm 8:5 says:

> *"You made him a little lower than…"*

Many translations say *"than the angels"* or *"heavenly beings."* Both of these translations are wrong. There are many translations that say, *"God,"* and that is correct. In the original Hebrew text it says, "Elohim." Elohim is the Hebrew name of the Creator God—God the Creator is Elohim. In Genesis chapter one, every time it says "God," it uses the Hebrew name "Elohim." So "Elohim" is the first name of God used in the Bible.

So what is the angel talking about in Psalm 8? He is talking about the Creator and His creation. Verse three says:

> *"When I consider your heavens, the work of your fingers, the moon and the stars…"*

Verse four asks:

> *"What is man…?"*

And then in verse five, he says:

> *"You made him a little lower than [Elohim, the Creator God]."*

What does that mean? Let's go back a little bit. First, there was God. He is the Most High. He is the Highest of the high, the Most High.

Then, the first beings God created were the angels. They were below Him. They were His servants.

Then one of those angels rebelled, whose name was Lucifer (now called satan). When he rebelled, a third of the angels rebelled with him, and they were cast out of heaven to the earth. They are called the fallen angels.

So there was God, then under Him were the angels, and then under them were the fallen angels. But when God created mankind, there was a new class! *"What is man? …You made him a little lower than [Elohim]."* So God created mankind just below Himself, but above the angels!

It is a lie (a Hollywood fictional story) that when people die, they become an angel. There is no promotion to the angelic class. You don't go to heaven and become an angel. That would be a demotion! No. We are created in a higher class, in the image of God!

Angels were created to be God's and our servants, as we read earlier in Hebrews 1:14:

> *"Are not all angels ministering spirits sent to serve those who will inherit salvation?"*

So God made mankind just below Himself, in His own likeness. The angels are not in His likeness, and the animals are not in His likeness. But mankind is created in His likeness, or you could say "of His own kind," not a different kind. So we are of God's kind, and our rank and position is just below God.

Authority

Let's go back to Genesis 1:26 (KJV):

> *"And God said, Let us make man in our image, after our likeness:* ***and let them have dominion*** *over the fish of the sea, and over the fowl of the air, and over the cattle, and over all the earth, and over every creeping thing that creepeth upon the earth."*

Notice the word "dominion." The dictionary defines dominion as "the power or right of governing and controlling; sovereign authority; rule; control." So you could also say, "Let them have authority."

This is something else that is different about mankind than any other creation. Angels do not have authority, except to do or say exactly what God commands them, and animals do not have authority. But mankind has authority over the earth.

> *"...**Let them have dominion** over the fish of the sea, and over the fowl of the air, and over the cattle, and **over all the earth**, and over every creeping thing that creepeth upon the earth."*

"Over all the earth" means the physical earth, including all the elements, such as water, fire, dirt, wind, minerals, oil, gas, and all plants and vegetation. So we have authority over the fish, birds, animals, and creeping things, and the physical earth and everything in it.

God said it again in Genesis 1:28 (KJV):

> *"And God blessed them, and God said unto them, Be fruitful, and multiply, and replenish the earth, **and subdue it: and have dominion** over the fish of the sea, and over*

> *the fowl of the air, and over every living thing that moveth upon the earth."*

The word "subdue" in the Hebrew means "to subject, subdue, force, keep under, bring into bondage, make subservient, dominate, tread down, subjugate."[2] Here again, it says we are supposed to subdue the earth and everything in it and make it subservient to our authority.

In Psalm 8:6–8 (AMPC), following verse five which says He made mankind a little lower than Elohim, it says again:

> [6] *"You made him to have dominion over the works of Your hands; You have put all things under his feet:* [7] *All sheep and oxen, yes, and the beasts of the field,* [8] *The birds of the air, and the fish of the sea, and whatever passes along the paths of the seas."*

The New Jerusalem Bible says in verse six, God made mankind *"lord"* over the works of His hands. So God created us to be lord and ruler over the earth, having dominion over the birds, fish, creatures, livestock, and all the physical earth.

Why are we supposed to rule over the animals, birds, and fish? To protect them and preserve them—not just feed them—by using our spiritual authority over the curse. Romans 8:19 (AMPC) says:

> *"For [even the whole] creation (all nature) waits expectantly and longs earnestly for God's sons to be made known [waits for the revealing, the disclosing of their sonship]."*

The creation is groaning (verse 22), waiting for the manifestation (KJV) and revealing of the sons of God—waiting for us to know who we are so that we can rule over the earth and take authority over the curse of sin and death.

That's why it's a lot easier to get results praying for hurt or sick animals than it is praying for people—because they don't doubt, they don't argue, and they don't have their own theology that God put sickness on them to teach them something! They are subject to our authority!

I've prayed for dogs more than once, and I saw them instantly healed. When I was in Malaita, Solomon Islands, I saw a dog that was crippled in his back legs because a tree fell on his backside. All he could do was drag himself along with his front paws. My heart went out to him, and the last day I was there, just before I left for the airport, I couldn't bear to see him that way any more, so I secretly went behind a building and prayed over that dog. I laid my hands on it and commanded the dog to be healed in Jesus' Name. Then I left. I returned to that village about six weeks later, and that dog was running! I asked one of the pastors, "When did that dog start running?" He said, "About the time you left, he was healed!" Praise God!

So you can pray for the animals, and that's what we're supposed to do when we see the curse of sickness, disease, or injury in them. We're supposed to set them free. We are here to rule over them for their protection, safety, and deliverance from the curse, and also to keep them from harming people. Luke 10:19 says:

> *"I have given you authority to trample on snakes and scorpions and to overcome all the power of the enemy; nothing will harm you."*

Psalm 91:13 says:

> *"You will tread upon the lion and the cobra; you will trample the great lion and the serpent."*

We can take authority over them when we see they are about to hurt someone. God has also given the animals to us for food, as He said in Genesis 9:3:

> *"Everything that lives and moves will be food for you. Just as I gave you the green plants, I now give you everything."*

That authority is for a set period of time. God gave mankind what we could call a lease to rule the earth. We are still in that period of time—the age of mankind—as we are still here working as men have since the beginning. However, when this time is up, things will change. That will take place when Jesus returns to earth at the end of the Tribulation to set up His Kingdom on earth, and then He will rule the earth sovereignly for a thousand years. Those of us who are born again[3] will continue to rule with Him, under His kingship.

The Glory

Let me ask you another question: When God made Adam, was Adam naked? No. He did not have physical clothes, but he did not need them. He was made in the image of God. Is God naked? No. Everything God made was clothed from the inside out. Birds are clothed with feathers, fish are clothed with scales, and animals are clothed with fur or hide. What is God clothed with? Glory! Psalm 104:1 (NAB) says:

> *"...You are clothed with majesty and glory"*

(see also Ezekiel 1:27–28; Ezekiel 8:2).

The glory of God is the life, light, and power of God. Life is light. Life is power. Light is power. Light is life. That glory radiates from within God and encompasses God.

Psalm 8:5 (NKJV) says:

> *"For You have made him a little lower than [Elohim], And You have crowned him with glory and honor."*

That crown was not just a little ring on his head. The word "crowned" in the original Hebrew text means "to surround, to encompass, to encircle, to close in, to crown."[4] The crowning of a king is also a robing—he gets a robe with the crown. So God's glory literally encompassed and surrounded man like it encompasses God! God's glory consumed man. He was made in the exact image of God, with the light and life of God dwelling in him just like it was dwelling in God. Adam himself was robed in glory!

The crowning would have been a magnificent spectacle! The crowning ceremony of a king is so grand and magnificent, with great pomp and show. To see God bring in this man—Adam—with everything in all creation—including the angels—

standing there watching as He then crowned His crowning glory on this man would have been magnificent!

Looking at Psalm 8:5 (NKJV) again, it says:

"...You have crowned him with glory ***and honor.****"*

This is something else to consider about honor. You cannot give honor to something or someone that is beneath you. We do not give honor to animals. You only give honor to something or someone on your level or above you. We love to say, "We give you glory, Lord. We give you honor. Glory and honor to the King of kings and the Lord of lords! We magnify you!" And rightly so.

But guess what God did on that day? He gave man glory and honor! Why could He do that? Only because mankind is made in God's image! God was saying, "Not only do you give Me glory and honor, but I also in turn give you glory and honor." By crowning man with glory and honor, He was saying, "You are not beneath me. I do not consider you beneath My feet. I consider you on My own level. I will talk to you face to face." Glory to God! Isn't that wonderful? Isn't that marvelous?

That glory was the lifeline between mankind and God. It was a spiritual umbilical cord that connected mankind to God, providing a continual flow of God's life and light into the man.

Chapter Three

Lost and Restored

Then something happened. There was a temptation. The devil, in the body of the serpent, came into the garden of Eden and deceived Eve. What was the temptation? The temptation was a deception. This is so amazing. Genesis 3:1 says:

> *"Now the serpent was more crafty than any of the wild animals the Lord God had made. He said to the woman, 'Did God really say, 'You must not eat from any tree in the garden'?"*

The Deception

Now look at Genesis 3:4–5:

> *"4 You will not certainly die,' the serpent said to the woman. 5 'For God knows that when*

you eat from it your eyes will be opened, ***and you will be like God****…'"*

That was the deception! He made her forget who she was. She was already like God! Mankind was made *in the image and likeness of God!* And the devil came along and said, "Do you want to be like God? You can be like God if you just don't do what He says and you eat this fruit." And she said, "Yes, I want to be like God."

Being like God is what satan wanted! That "God-likeness" was what Lucifer was after, and it was the very thing he was cast out of heaven for! Isaiah 14:12–15 say:

> [12] *"How you have fallen from heaven, O morning star* [that is satan, called Lucifer before he was cast out of heaven], *son of the dawn! You have been cast down to the earth, you who once laid low the nations!* [13] *You said in your heart, 'I will ascend to the heavens; I will raise my throne above the stars of God; I will sit enthroned on the mount of assembly, on the utmost heights of Mount Zaphon [mount of assembly in the uttermost north*—AMPC*].* [14] *I will ascend above the tops of the clouds;* ***I will make myself like the Most High****.'* [15] *But you are*

> *brought down to the realm of the dead, to the depths of the pit [to Sheol (Hades), to the innermost recesses of the pit (the region of the dead)*—AMPC*]."*

Satan wanted the position, authority, and glory that were given to mankind! He wanted to be like the Most High! But he didn't have the right to be like the Most High. He started an insurrection against God to take that place, but it got him kicked out of heaven. Then God made mankind in His likeness—giving mankind the position, authority, and glory—and the devil was standing there watching, and he turned green with jealousy and envy. He was thinking, "What are you doing? You are making mankind in Your image. Why didn't you make me in Your image? I want to be in Your image. I want that position, authority, and glory!" And he became jealous of mankind for the "God-likeness" and the position, authority, and glory that were given to mankind that he himself could never have. So, what did he do? He designed a plot to steal it away from the one who had it!

He went to Eve in the garden of Eden and deceived her. Adam was right there with her. Genesis 3:6 says:

> *"When the woman saw that the fruit of the tree was good for food and pleasing to the eye,*

and also desirable for gaining wisdom, she took some and ate it. She also gave some to her husband, who was with her, and he ate it."

He was not on the other side of the garden. He was right there with her, and they both ate the fruit that God told them not to eat. They ate the fruit trying to become like God, either not realizing or forgetting that they were already like God! If satan can make you forget who you are and what God has given you, then he can steal it from you!

High Treason

That act of disobedience was an act of high treason. Do you know what treason is? Treason is disloyalty to and betrayal of your nation, your government, or your lord. Treason is breaking loyalty to the one to whom you owe allegiance and helping the enemy.

God made mankind in His own image and gave him everything. Man owed everything to God. But instead, he committed treason. He betrayed God through disobedience and turned and followed the enemy of God. When Adam and Eve obeyed satan and followed him, they committed high treason, and satan became their new lord! Romans 6:16 says:

> *"Don't you know that when you offer yourselves to someone as obedient slaves, you are slaves of the one you obey—whether you are slaves to sin, which leads to death, or to obedience, which leads to righteousness?"*

Adam was in his high position just below God. Then he turned and obeyed the temptation of satan, and he fell, fell, fell, fell, fell, fell—below the angels and below the fallen angels! A fallen angel—satan—became his new lord, and he immediately became a slave! A slave to satan, to sin, and to the curse of sin and death! (see also Galatians 4:8)

When Adam sinned, he gave his authority, dominion, and his lordship over the earth to the one whom he obeyed. He submitted himself and became subject to satan, and satan became the lord, ruler, and master over the earth and over the human race. Second Corinthians 4:4 calls satan "the god of this world." Satan was not created the god of this world. He was cast down from heaven to earth as a fallen angel. But he became the god of this world when Adam gave him his authority.

Man could do nothing about it now. Even the animals, who were once under man's authority, had the power to rise up and devour man. He was powerless, he was in slavery, he was in bondage, he was in darkness, he was in death—spiritual death.

In that same act of disobedience, mankind lost the glory of God. Romans 3:23 says:

> *"for all have sinned and* ***fall short of the glory of God.****"*

The glory departed! The light went out! That life that was in him was sucked out of him like a vacuum. Instantly, the light became darkness. The life became death. Love became hate. Joy became sorrow. Peace became turmoil. Faith became fear…and he hid from God.

His glory robe was gone! That's when he saw he was naked. That's when he was exposed in sin. He had fallen from the glory! He was then in darkness! The umbilical cord of life that connected mankind to God was cut off, and he was connected to his new master—satan—and spiritual death entered him! He had lost everything God had given him!

I can imagine satan taunting God: "What are you going to do now? What are you going to do now? What are you going to do now? He's mine. I've got him! I've got your precious man! He's mine!"

God's Secret Plan

God was left on the outside looking in, watching the loss of His man. He saw that His relationship with mankind was broken. He saw that His son made in His image was now the captive of the enemy. So what was He going to do?

First Corinthians 2:7–8 say;

> [7] *"No, we declare God's wisdom,* ***a mystery that has been hidden*** *and* ***that God destined for our glory before time began.*** (NIV)
> [7] *"But we give the news of* ***the secret wisdom of God****, which he had kept in store before the world came into existence,* ***for our glory;*** (BBE)
> [8] *None of the rulers of this age understood it, for if they had, they would not have crucified the Lord of glory."* (NIV)

The word "mystery" in the Greek (the New Testament was written in Greek) means "secret;

hidden thing."[5] The New English Translation (NET) in verse 7 says:

> *"Instead we speak the wisdom of God, hidden in a mystery, that God determined before the* **ages** *for our glory."*

It was a mystery hidden in God from before the foundation of the world!

The word "ages" in the original Greek text is the word "aion" from which we get the word "eon." It literally means "forever, eternity, ages."[6]

It was God's secret wisdom, like there was a box on the inside of God saying, "Top Secret!" God had a plan for mankind before eternity began, *and it was for our glory*! He knew mankind would fall, and He had a plan! Oh, what a plan, and oh, what a Planner!

So what did He do? God began speaking the Word right there in Genesis chapter three. He spoke the first prophetic word about Jesus in Genesis 3:15, saying:

> *"And I will put enmity between you and the woman, and between your offspring and hers; he will crush your head, and you will strike his heel."*

That was the first prophecy that the Messiah, the Christ, Jesus would come and defeat satan! For the next four thousand years, God continued to speak through the prophets saying, "The Messiah, the Savior of the world, is coming! The Savior of the world is coming!"

Finally, as it says in John 1:14,

> ***"The Word*** [all those prophetic words] ***became flesh*** *and made his dwelling among us. We have seen his glory, the glory of the one and only Son, who came from the Father, full of grace and truth."*

Galatians 4:4–5 say:

> [4] *"But when the set time had fully come, God sent his Son, born of a woman, born under the law,* [5] *to redeem those under the law, that we might receive adoption to sonship."*

His plan was for our redemption and restoration! In the fullness of time, God sent His Son and redeemed mankind—freeing him from the power of satan, and sin, and the curse of sin and death and restoring to mankind all that he had lost!

The Restoration

First, we are brought back into relationship with our Creator God. Second Corinthians 5:18–19 say God was reconciling the world to Himself in Christ:

> [18] *"All this is from God, who reconciled us to himself through Christ and gave us the ministry of reconciliation: [19] that God was reconciling the world to himself in Christ, not counting men's sins against them. And he has committed to us the message of reconciliation."*

Ephesians 2:13 says:

> *"But now in Christ Jesus you who once were far away have been brought near by the blood of Christ."*

We are united with Him again, as it says in John 17:21:

> *"that all of them may be one, Father, just as you are in me and I am in you. May they also be in us…"*

And John 14:20 says:

> *"On that day you will realize that I am in my Father, and you are in me, and I am in you."*

Colossians 3:3 says:

> *"For you died, and your life is now hidden with Christ in God."*

The umbilical cord of life with the Father God is reconnected! Hallelujah!

Second, now we are no longer slaves to satan and sin. Galatians 4:7 (NKJV) says:

> *"Therefore you are no longer a slave but a son, and if a son, then an heir of God through Christ."*

Romans 6:17–18 say:

> *17 "But thanks be to God that, though you used to be slaves to sin, you have come to obey from your heart the pattern of teaching that has now claimed your allegiance. 18* ***You have been set free from sin*** *and have become slaves to righteousness."*

Wow! Praise God! We have been set free from sin! It no longer has authority over us!

Third, in Christ Jesus we are reborn and recreated *in the image of God.* Second Corinthians 5:17 (NKJV) says:

> *"Therefore, if anyone is in Christ, he is a new creation; old things have passed away; behold, all things have become new."*

The New Living Translation (NLT) says:

> *"This means that anyone who belongs to Christ has become a new person. The old life is gone; a new life has begun!"*

Praise the Lord!

Remember the word "image"? Colossians 3:9–10 say:

> 9 *"...since you have taken off your old self with its practices* 10 *and have put on the new self, which is being renewed in knowledge in the* ***image*** *of its Creator."*

And Ephesians 4:24 says:

> *"...put on the new self,* **created to be like God** *in true righteousness and holiness."*

The new self is *"created to be like God!"* We are in His image and likeness again! Hallelujah!

Fourth, Ephesians 2:4–6 say:

> [4] *"But because of his great love for us, God, who is rich in mercy,* [5] *made us alive with Christ even when we were dead in transgressions—it is by grace you have been saved.* [6] *And God* ***raised us up with Christ and seated us with him in the heavenly realms*** *in Christ Jesus."*

What does that mean? He gave us our position back! Hallelujah! That is *not after* we get to heaven. Some people say, "When we get to heaven, we will be raised up with Christ." No, it's now. It is when we are born again[3] and recreated in His image. At that moment, He raises us up. We are *now* spiritually seated with Christ in heavenly places!

We need to remember our position. We need to remember that the devil is under our feet. You could write "devil" on the bottom of your shoe just to remind yourself that that is where he is. He's down there. We are seated with Christ in heavenly places. *Now*, in Christ Jesus, we have regained our position!

Fifth, our authority is restored. Jesus said in Luke 10:19:

> *"I have given you authority to trample on snakes and scorpions and to overcome all the power of the enemy…"*

He said in Matthew 18:18:

> *"Truly I tell you, whatever you bind on earth will be bound in heaven, and whatever you loose on earth will be loosed in heaven."*

He said (my paraphrase), "In My Name, cast out demons. In My Name, heal the sick and raise the dead" (Matthew 10:8; Mark 16:17–19).

What does that mean? He gave us *His* authority in *His* Name.

Jesus took back from the devil what was rightfully ours. The devil stole it, but in Christ, we have been given the authority back. That's why we have the right to use the Name of Jesus. That's why we have the right to bind satan. That's why we have the right to rebuke him and cast him out. That's why we have the right to rule in Jesus' Name!

Sixth, our glory is restored!

Hebrews 2:9 says:

> *"But we do see Jesus, who was made lower than the angels for a little while…"*

There the word "angels" is correct because He had to become like us in our fallen state. We fell below the angels, so He had to be made below the angels.

> [9] *"But we do see Jesus, who was made lower than the angels for a little while,* ***now crowned with glory and honor*** *because he suffered death, so that by the grace of God he might taste death for everyone."*

In verse ten it says, *"In bringing many sons* ***to glory****…"* So in Christ Jesus, God has brought many sons back to glory! When he was raised up in glory, we are raised up in glory!

Romans 9:23–24 say:

> *"What if he did this to make the riches of his glory known to the objects of his mercy,* ***whom he prepared in advance for glory,—***[24]***even us****, whom he also called…"*

This says He prepared us in advance for glory!

Second Corinthians 3:18 (ESV) says:

> *"And we all, with unveiled face, beholding the glory of the Lord, are being transformed into the same* ***image*** *from one degree of glory to another. For this comes from the Lord who is the Spirit."*

The King James Version says:

> *"But we all, with open face beholding as in a glass the glory of the Lord, are* ***changed into the same image from glory to glory****, even as by the Spirit of the Lord."*

Here we see that we are again made into His likeness and image from glory to glory!

First Corinthians 2:7 again says:

> *"No, we declare God's wisdom,* ***a mystery that has been hidden*** *and* ***that God destined for our glory before time began.****"*

The Amplified Bible says:

> *"…**for our glorification**, to lift us into the glory of His presence."*

This mystery hidden in God from before the foundation of the world was to bring mankind back into His presence, image, and likeness and to raise us back into the position, authority, and glory that we had with Him before man fell in sin! Hallelujah! Praise the Lord! Glory to God!

Our Future

And God's plan for us does not stop there! Ephesians 2:7 says:

> *"in order that in the coming ages [eons] he might* ***show*** *the* ***incomparable*** *riches of his grace, expressed in his kindness to us in Christ Jesus."*

The Wuest translation (The New Testament: An Expanded Translation) says:

> *"In order that He might* ***exhibit*** *for His own glory in the ages that will* ***pile themselves one upon another in continuous succession,*** *the* ***surpass-ing*** *wealth of His grace in (acts of) kindness to us in Christ Jesus."*

And the Amplified Bible says it like this:

> *"He did this that He might clearly* ***demonstrate*** *through the ages to come* ***the immeasurable (limitless, surpassing) riches of His free grace*** *(His unmerited favor) in His kindness and goodness of heart toward us in Christ Jesus."*

Wow! God's plan for us, starting now, is that through the coming ages—age after age piled one upon another—He will show, exhibit, and demonstrate the incomparable, surpassing, limitless, and immeasurable riches of His free grace and acts of kindness toward us!

Jeremiah 29:11 says:

> *"'For I know the plans I have for you,' declares the Lord, 'plans to prosper you and not to harm you, plans to give you hope and a future.'"*

God's plans are to do great and marvelous things for us—now and through the ages to come! Hallelujah!

So what is *The Story of God's Glorious Plan for Man*? It is that mankind was made in God's image and glory, and then he fell from that glory. But now in Christ Jesus, we are recreated in His likeness and image, we are restored to our position and authority, we are brought back into glory, and we will spend a gloriously bright future with Him through the eternal ages to come! Hallelujah! The cycle is complete!

Prayer for Salvation

Romans 10:9–11 say, *"if you confess with your mouth, 'Jesus is Lord,' and believe in your heart that God raised him from the dead, you will be saved. [10] For it is with your heart that you believe and are justified, and it is with your mouth that you confess and are saved. [11] As the Scripture says, 'Anyone who trusts in him will never be put to shame.'"*

1 John 1:9 says, *"If we confess our sins, he is faithful and just and will forgive us our sins and purify us from all unrighteousness."*

If you have never asked Jesus to be the Lord of your life, you can pray this prayer:

"Dear Lord Jesus, I know I am a sinner. Please forgive me of my sins and come into my heart and life. You said in Romans 10:9, "If you confess with your mouth, 'Jesus is Lord,' and believe in your heart that God raised him from the dead, you will be saved." So I confess that You, Jesus, are my Lord and Savior, and I believe in my heart that You are the Son of God, You died on the cross for my sins, and God raised You from the dead. Now I give You my life. Please teach me Your ways and help me to serve You all of my life. Thank you for saving me and cleansing me of sin, and making me your child. I give You praise, in Jesus' Name, Amen!"

Notes:

[1] For more information and study on how much God loves us, read my book *God Loves Me.*

[2] Strong, James. *Strong's Exhaustive Concordance of the Bible.* Abingdon Press, 1890.
(Hebrew dictionary) 3533

[3] Born again: John 3:3–6 (NKJV) say:

> [3] *"Jesus answered and said to him, 'Most assuredly, I say to you, unless one is born again, he cannot see the kingdom of God.'* [4] *Nicodemus said to Him, 'How can a man be born when he is old? Can he enter a second time into his mother's womb and be born?'* [5] *Jesus answered, 'Most assuredly, I say to you, unless one is born of water and the Spirit, he cannot enter the kingdom of God.* [6] *That which is born of the flesh is flesh, and that which is born of the Spirit is spirit.'"*

Also, 1 Peter 1:21,23 say:

> [21] *"Through him you believe in God, who raised him from the dead and glorified him, and so your faith and hope are in God.* [23] *For you have been born again, not of perishable seed, but of imperishable, through the living and enduring word of God."*

Being born again means your spirit is made new (you are a new creation on the inside—2 Corinthians 5:17) when you believe in and receive Jesus Christ as your personal Savior, and you are born into God's family becoming one of His children. See the prayer for salvation to be born again!

[4] Strong's (Hebrew) 5849

[5] Strong's (Greek) *3466*

[6] Strong's (Greek) *165*

MORE BOOKS BY CHERRI CAMPBELL

Adventures with Jesus—A Journal of My World Missionary Travels

God Loves Me

The Baptism in the Holy Spirit & The Benefits of Speaking in Tongues

Go to victoriousfaith.co

About the Author

By jumbo jet and small propeller plane, by ship, small boat, ferry and train, by truck, bus, jeepney, auto rickshaw, automobile, motorcycle, tricycle, and by foot, **Cherri Campbell** has been a traveling missionary in over twenty nations, teaching the Word of God and preaching in Bible schools, ministers' conferences, churches, youth conferences, and women's conferences. She is the author of a one-year Bible school curriculum called *Foundations of Victorious Living*, which has been adopted by several Bible schools. She has lived in the bush in Vanuatu, the Solomon Islands, Papua New Guinea, and the Federated States of Micronesia. She has preached and taught the Word of God in the underground church in Asia, traveled by train preaching across India, taught in conferences in the Himalayas, and preached in Bible schools, churches, and conferences in Southeast Asia, East Africa, and West Africa.

Cherri now lives in Colorado, and in 2013, she began a daily half-hour radio broadcast called *Victorious Faith*, which is also available on her website, *victoriousfaith.co*, and YouTube channel. Her simple yet in-depth teaching style has helped many Christians around the world, including pastors, gain a deeper understanding and practical application of the Word of God to receive healings, supernatural provision, victories, and breakthroughs in their own lives.

Cherri's calling is to train and equip the Body of Christ to live and operate *victoriously* in the Kingdom of God, maturing the saints to *be* a glorious and triumphant Church and to *do* the works of Jesus Christ.

www.ingramcontent.com/pod-product-compliance
Lightning Source LLC
LaVergne TN
LVHW010108110826
845155LV00028B/536

* 9 7 8 1 9 5 1 8 0 0 0 0 0 *